THEN & NOW

RUSSIAN RIVER

RUSSIAN RIVER

John C. Schubert and
Valerie A. Munthe

John Schubert: Dedicated to my granddaughters—Jasmine, Sabrina, Johnna, and Heather. May they carry on the passion for their community, their culture, and their own history.

Valerie Munthe: This book and all its memories are dedicated to my children, Atreyu and Jadziah. Remember: in the dark dampness of the redwood forest sprang the roots of our family, nourished by our beloved river.

ON THE FRONT COVER: This *c.* 1910 photograph, looking upstream toward Roland's Beach from Johnson's Beach, is of the first Guerneville Bridge, built of wood in 1885. (Photograph by Valerie Munthe; collection of John C. Schubert.)

ON THE BACK COVER: Dubrava Beach, shown here in 1940, was and continues to be a very popular beach amongst the local and visiting youth. (Collection of John C. Schubert.)

Contents

ACKNOWLEDGMENTS

This book would not have come to its fruition if it were not for the personal histories of the Russian River residents and their willingness to welcome us into their lives. The authors would like to express their combined thanks to those who shared their knowledge and memories of living "on the river": Jane Barry, Herbert Angelo Genelly, Clare Harris, Laura Wilson, Tony Hoskins, Laura Parent, Ben Larner, Sam and Opal Pullaro, Frank and Nancy Lambert, and Elenor Twohy; a large thank you to all.

Though I have been a student of Russian River history for over 50 years, there were others who were the trailblazers before me. They pushed me on—most notably the late Guerneville natives and writers Jack Hetzel and Raymond Clar.
—John C. Schubert

I would like to thank my family and dear friends for their encouragement, support, advice, information, comic relief, and inspiration, but in particular, my husband, Jesse, for his unwavering love and support. Also deserving thanks are all the generous residents who allowed us on their premises and Mother Nature for creating such adventurous obstacles for the "now" photographs with her newly regenerated forests.
—Valerie Munthe

In courtesy lines, "photograph by" refers to the modern image, and "collection of" indicates the historical photograph.

INTRODUCTION

The Russian River, known to the natives as Shabaikai (sha-beh-keh; "the snake"), twists and turns its 100-mile length into the Pacific Ocean through the low-lying mountains of Sonoma County in Northern California. Along the way are the small towns that make up one of California's favorite vacation communities—the Russian River Resort Area.

The area represented by the Russian River Chamber of Commerce and Visitor Center extends along the Russian River and includes several small, unincorporated communities. The largest of these towns is Guerneville, located 70 miles north of San Francisco, 16 miles northwest of Santa Rosa (the county seat), and approximately 15 miles east of the Pacific Ocean. The vicinity has historically been a resort and second home area and is dominated by commercial recreation uses as well as an up-and-coming popular winery appellation. This area is known worldwide, with many visitors coming from Europe, Australia, Canada, and the East Coast of the United States, and is regarded as one of the most beautiful vacation regions in the country. For the past few decades, the trend has been toward developing year-round habitation.

The Russian River area, comprised of narrow valley flatlands dominated by steep surrounding hillsides, is covered with mixed forest growth—including redwood, madrone, and laurel, which is also known as bay, myrtlewood, or pepperwood. With elevations of the surrounding ridges varying from 600 to 1,000 feet, these slopes, when combined with unstable soils and difficult access, limit potential development, while valley flatlands are subject to periodic flooding from the Russian River and surrounding creeks. The rich soils are comprised of ancient forest mulch and flood silt deposits and, when paired with mild weather, create the optimal opportunity for growing any type of vegetable or fruit (with the exception of tropical fruits, such as pineapples and bananas). This unique natural development also allows for perfect conditions for the growing of wine and champagne grapes.

Russian River has gone through several changes in its more than 150 years of modern history. The original inhabitants of the region, Pomo Indians, lived on the land during the summer months and traveled the narrow trails that linked the eastern oak-donned hills with the coastal encampments. It was not until the early 1800s that foreign visitors began trickling into this hidden region. Russian fur trappers paddled east on what they called Slavianka ("little Russian girl"), later to be called Russian River. The Russian settlers are responsible for the steep decline and eventual eradication of the local beaver and river otter population; however, because of their brief encounter with the Pomo Indians, the Great Museum of Anthropology and Ethnography (Kunstkamera) in St. Petersburg, Russia, houses the world's largest collection of Pomo Indian baskets. The first American settlers to this area established their homesteads in the small clearings scattered in the redwood forest. Shortly after, the lumber mills followed, slowly cutting their way toward the heart of the forest. The first mill in the Guerneville area was established on the north side in what was then the tallest forest on Earth, with the tallest tree holding that record in the Guinness Book of World Records at one time. The area was called "Big Bottom" due to a geographic feature that created a bowl effect around what is now Guerneville.

To help ship out the tremendous volume of cut wood and lumber, a standard-gage railroad was built from San Rafael through Santa Rosa, with a branch traveling west to Guerneville. This branch line was completed by 1877, and by around 1905 the Guerneville branch continued west and connected with the narrow-gage railroad in Monte Rio. Due to financial hardship during the Great Depression, the railroad company pulled out the narrow gage in 1933 and then the standard gage in 1935.

From the late 1800s through the early 20th century, the thinning of the forest created open land for homes and agriculture, allowing established families the use of the rich soils for private vegetable gardens, orchards, and animal husbandry. These private farms eventually turned into apple and prune orchards, hop fields, award-winning tobacco fields, and present-day champagne vineyards, all of which yielded important crops contributing to the area's economy. Eventually the economic base for timber became exhausted and was supplanted by tourism, with vacationers coming from the San Francisco Bay Area to the newly developed summer homes and resorts. During these early decades, the logging railroad also provided access to the Russian River area for tourists, vacationers, and residents alike. Throughout the 1920s, the Russian River Resort Area roared with passenger trains filled with eager vacationers traveling to towns like Hacienda, Summerhome Park, Rio Nido, Guerneville, Guernewood Park, Monte Rio, Villa Grande, Duncans Mills, and Jenner. Tourists flocked to these small communities for the activities on the river, such as canoeing, swimming, hunting, fishing, and live music and dances. Each town had something unique to offer, represented in its motto: Monte Rio's was, and is to this day, "Vacation Wonderland"; Rio Nido's was "Memories that Linger"; and Guerneville's is "The Heart of the Russian River." Monte Rio was also famous for the Montrio Hotel, the first building in Sonoma County to have an elevator, which ran from the ground floor to its seventh floor.

The area experienced its peak of activity from the 1920s through World War II, with an influx of big band music, nightly dances, and annual events such as the Pageant of Fire Mountain, Stumptown Daze Parade, Monte Rio Water Carnival, and bowling tournaments, to name a few. During the war years, the Russian River Resort Area was the closest vacation spot to San Francisco and did not shut down until late autumn. Consequently, military personnel made it boom night and day, since it was the last chance for them to let their hair down before being shipped out to the Pacific theater.

From the 1950s through the 1970s, as light industry grew in the Santa Rosa Valley and more became involved in the expanding wine industry, more substantial homes were built in the river region. During the 1970s and 1980s, many gay residents of San Francisco became inspired by the area's natural beauty and helped to revive many of the businesses. By the beginning of the 1980s, many of the resorts were revitalized, repaired, and rebuilt. Although known worldwide by visitors near and far, in some regards the area has become part of Santa Rosa and San Francisco's bedroom communities. People who have chosen to retire here and those who have found it an ideal atmosphere in which to raise families have come to cherish the natural beauty of the redwoods and the Russian River.

Although there are not nearly as many amenities as there were when the river area was roaring, there still remains a draw of visitors who explore the Russian River Valley for its fun recreation, ancient redwoods at Armstrong Woods, and world-renowned wines and champagnes. The people who live in and visit this region tend to feel a deep connection with surrounding nature, the people, and their own personal history therein. Many have vacationed here as children with their families or grew up in the various family businesses that hosted the tourist boom each season. Given this unique opportunity to reflect on the changes of these hometowns, it is our purpose to give these people something solid to remind them about what it is they love now and what they treasured then about the Russian River.

CHAPTER 1

UPPER RESORT

HACIENDA, SUMMERHOME PARK, HILTON, KORBEL, RIO NIDO

The forest in this area, known as Summerhome Park, was cleared out in the 1880s, as depicted in this *c.* 1905 postcard. After logging ceased, the land was converted to agricultural use and, in 1908, Summerhome Park Company was formed to sell and develop lots for vacation use. Typical of this early summer vacation area were tent cabins and tent platforms. (Collection of John C. Schubert.)

11

This *c.* 1900 postcard shows a northeast view of the railroad bridge at Hacienda. The area on the west side of the bridge was formerly called "Cosmo," while Forest Hills lies on the east side. In 1914, this span was replaced by a steel railroad bridge and, after the railroad was removed in 1935, was converted into a one-lane automobile bridge. Then in 1950, Sonoma County funded a bridge-widening project, creating the two-lane structure seen today. (Photograph by Jesse Munthe; collection of John C. Schubert.)

North Western Pacific R. R. Bridge,
Cosmo, California

Clay deposits discovered around 1885 were developed for making bricks and terra cotta drainpipes and became known as the Hilton Brick Yard. This real photo postcard, taken in 1907, shows a view facing south toward the Russian River. The train stopped here to pick up loaded boxcars for shipment to the outside world. The brick industry shut down in 1912, and the buildings were torn down; afterward, the district slowly developed into a residential and camping area. (Photograph by Valerie Munthe; collection of John C. Schubert.)

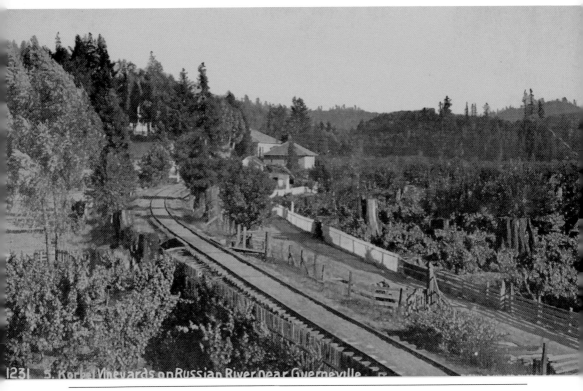

Looking east along the railroad tracks—now the site of River Road, which closely follows the original railroad bed—is a view of Korbel Champagne Cellars from around 1910. The Korbel Winery, established in 1880, is a world-renowned champagne producer. The earlier photograph shows a typical conversion of logged-over land into agricultural use, in this case vineyards, hops, and tobacco. Due to the growth of trees, the modern image was taken from a different angle. (Photograph by Valerie Munthe; collection of John C. Schubert.)

Taken around 1920, this photograph of Esterville, looking south, shows the Russian River at the Odd Fellows Summer Bridge that is still used today as a summer crossing. This crossing connects Korbel and River Road traffic to Esterville, Odd Fellows Park, and Highway 116 in Pocket Canyon. At this spot can be seen year-to-year changes that the river makes in the immediate landscape. (Photograph by Jesse Munthe; collection of John C. Schubert.)

RUSSIAN RIVER BRIDGE AT ESTERVILLE

The photograph, taken in 1909, is facing north from the railroad tracks into Eagle's Nest. In 1910, the name was changed to Rio Nido, Spanish for "river nest." The area was developed and expanded greatly during the 1930s. The modern view shows the hub and commercial center of Rio Nido, which includes the Rio Nido Roadhouse and public pool. (Photograph by Valerie Munthe; collection of John C. Schubert.)

This picture shows another northern view from River Road at Rio Nido looking into the commercial center. Today the Rio Nido Roadhouse and public pool are what remains of the neighborhood commerce. Rio Nido does, as it always has, receive a vast array of visitors, like this motorcycle group of about 200 riders, as seen in this modern photograph. (Photograph by Valerie Munthe; collection of John C. Schubert.)

Taken in 1927, this photograph shows the Rio Nido Hotel, built in 1918 by Guy "English" Smith, an Englishman (hence the Tudor architecture). The open-air theater is immediately behind the photographer. This building is the last of the original structures in the center of downtown Rio Nido and had recently been renovated and converted for office spaces as well as theatrical stage productions, courtesy of the Pegasus Theater. (Photograph by Valerie Munthe; collection of John C. Schubert.)

This image is looking northeast at Rio Nido's main intersections, with River Road to the right of the photographer. The road straight ahead and up the hill is today's Memory Lane, and the road that swings to the left, known today as Canyon Two Road, is the entrance into central Rio Nido. The *c.* 1930 photograph depicts the Rio Nido Real Estate office. (Photograph by Valerie Munthe; collection of John C. Schubert.)

One of the best locations for a spectacular view of the Russian River is Memory Lane, which runs up a steep hillside just above River Road and empties into Canyon One Road. The older photograph, looking west, shows the newly constructed vacation bungalows of one of the many Rio Nido resorts in 1930. These summer cabins eventually became year-round residential rentals. (Photograph by Jesse Munthe; collection of John C. Schubert.)

The summer bands that performed in the dance pavilion would also give performances outside on the stage shown in this *c.* 1938 photograph. Behind the stage is the Rio Nido Grill and Bar and perched above the grill is the fondly remembered "Winking Moon" that was lit during summer evenings. The area today is now the Rio Nido Roadhouse and a public pool. (Photograph by Jesse Munthe; collection of John C. Schubert.)

This *c.* 1940 image shows an eastern view of the main entrance to Rio Nido along an unpaved River Road. The open-air Rio Nido Train Station, to the left, was later converted into a café and soda fountain. The building in the center was formerly known as Froehlich's Real Estate and remains a real estate office today. (Photograph by Jesse Munthe; collection of John C. Schubert.)

Looking upstream at what was once the Rio Nido Beach, signs of Mother Nature are prevalent. The Rio Nido Beach was one of three of the most popular beaches along the Russian River. Every season, the site was prepared by grating the gravel and sand for the concession stand and boat-rental office. Since the spot has not been used as a public beach since the 1980s, trees now present have been able to grow undisturbed. (Photograph by Jesse Munthe; collection of John C. Schubert.)

SCENE ON RUSSIAN RIVER
RIO NIDO, CAL

The Pennant Cottages in this *c.* 1933 photograph was a popular river resort. Facing east on what is today's Old River Road, this was the vehicle and pedestrian access to Guerneville. Out of sight to the right is the old railroad right-of-way, today's River Road. It is a commercial area now popularly known as the Rio Nido Strip. (Photograph by Valerie Munthe; collection of John C. Schubert.)

A snapshot of Roland's Beach in the early 1950s depicts another very popular public strand that was considered "ideal for young and old." Located halfway between Rio Nido and Guerneville on the North Bank of the Russian River, today it is the pickup site for Burke's Canoe Trips, a very popular tourist activity. (Photograph by Valerie Munthe; collection of John C. Schubert.)

Looking down the Russian River, Guerneville, Cal.

One of the first beaches to be developed for public use about 1905 was Johnson's Beach. This view, looking downriver from the historic 1923 Guerneville Bridge, has hardly changed since the first bridge was constructed in 1885. This public beach has been a destination for many generations of local residents and visitors alike. (Photograph by Jesse Munthe; collection of John C. Schubert.)

CHAPTER 2

HEART OF THE RIVER

GUERNEVILLE AND GUERNEWOOD PARK

Guerneville, as shown in the *c.* 1950s photograph, was and continues to be the largest town on the Russian River. Established in 1865, and formerly known as "Stumptown," Guerneville serves as a main hub of activities, lodging, and shopping for tourists, vacationers, and residents. (Collection of John C. Schubert.)

This *c.* 1910 photograph, looking upstream toward Roland's Beach from Johnson's Beach, shows the first Guerneville Bridge, built of wood in 1885. The development of summer homes and year-round residences has spread along both riverbanks, as seen here on the right, as has the growth of the surrounding forest, made possible when local lumber mills closed. (Photograph by Valerie Munthe; collection of John C. Schubert.)

ON THE RUSSIAN RIVER GUERNEVILLE CAL.

This photograph of State Highway 12 was taken in 1927, looking east at an area known as "Pocket Canyon." The original concrete highway, built in 1920, is still visible under the current asphalt layer. Today this is State Highway 116, which connects Guerneville to Jenner, Forestville, and Sebastopol. The Applewood Inn, once known as the Belden House, is best known for fine dining and exquisite lodging. (Photograph by Valerie Munthe; collection of John C. Schubert.)

The occasional high waters of the river rose again during the 1960s at the famous Pee Wee Golf, located at the south end of both Guerneville Bridges. Built in 1948 by Bill Koplin Sr. and managed by the family, Pee Wee Golf remains another well-known Russian River landmark to this day. (Photograph by Valerie Munthe; collection of John C. Schubert.)

HEART OF THE RIVER: GUERNEVILLE AND GUERNEWOOD PARK

The first Guerneville Bridge was a wooden structure built in 1885 and used by foot traffic, horse-drawn wagons, stagecoaches, and later, automobiles. The original bridge was replaced with a concrete structure in 1923. In 1998, a new state highway bridge was completed roughly 50 yards upstream. The old bridge was designated a historical landmark and pedestrian bridge. (Photograph by Valerie Munthe; collection of John C. Schubert.)

The 1938 photograph is a view of local businesses looking west along First Street in downtown Guerneville. Bicycling was, and continues to be, a popular recreational activity in the Russian River area. The same building now houses the Russian River Chamber of Commerce and Visitor Center, Russian River Art Gallery, and Andorno's Pizza Café. (Photograph by Valerie Munthe; collection of John C. Schubert.)

A westbound train from Santa Rosa is arriving in Guerneville in this *c.* 1898 photograph. After the tracks were removed in 1935, the railway bed formed the base of Main Street, also known as State Highway 116. Noel Tunstall, who operated the last scheduled stagecoach from Guerneville to Cazadero, owned the livery stable to the right. It was torn down in 1940 and is now the site of the Downtown Guerneville Plaza. (Photograph by Valerie Munthe; collection of John C. Schubert.)

This *c.* 1950 photograph, looking west, is of a bustling downtown Guerneville during the Stumptown Days festivities (hence the flags). The Guerneville Pharmacy building burned down in the 1963 fire, and a new edifice was erected in its place, which now houses Trio Restaurant. Bridgeway Restaurant is now the Guerneville Mercantile. Across the street, The Stork Club was once a popular bar; it is now a popular gay pub known as the Rainbow Cattle Company. The Louvre building housed Russian River Video for 25 years, and now Community First Credit Union. To the right, Russian River Realty remains. (Photograph by Valerie Munthe; collection of John C. Schubert.)

This is a view of the intersection of First Street and Armstrong Woods Road in downtown Guerneville from the perspective of the Guerneville Bridge. The Rochdale was built in 1905 and was the site of what is now currently the Guerneville Mercantile, built in 1957. Tunstall's Livery, to the right, was damaged during the 1906 earthquake. Where it stood are now the Guerneville Downtown Plaza and a bus stop. (Photograph by Valerie Munthe; collection of John C. Schubert.)

During the flood of 1955 (Guerneville floods roughly every 10 years), the Rexall Drug Store (now Guerneville Mercantile), Buchanan's (now Trio Restaurant), the Food Center, Ferenz's Sport Shop, and the Grove Theater barely escaped the waters of the Russian River. The latter three businesses burned in the fire of 1963. The Grove site is now the parking lot for Lark's Drugs. The building with the "Guerneville Pharmacy" sign was the former Odd Fellows Lodge. (Photograph by Valerie Munthe; collection of John C. Schubert.)

The old Guerneville School, built in 1923, was dedicated by the Masonic Lodge no. 272 in 1924 and served the local children until 1949 when it was relocated 1 mile north on Armstrong Woods Road. The windows, from left to right, are the fifth and sixth grades, seventh and eighth grades, the principal's office to the left of the entrance, and the girls' restroom to the right. This structure is now the Veteran's Hall and Sonoma County Sheriff Substation. (Photograph by Valerie Munthe; collection of John C. Schubert.)

Looking east up Main Street in 1937, two years after the railroad tracks were pulled up from the roadbed, this photograph shows the old Standard Station, now the KWIK Stop, and the old hardware store, now Main Street Station Pizzeria. The Owl Tavern and Associated Gas is now the location of Guerneville Liquors. Most of the block across the street was destroyed in the 1963 fire. (Photograph by Jesse Munthe; collection of John C. Schubert.)

Around 1916, the office of the Russian River Water Company was located at the southwest corner of Main and Church Streets, now the location of the Prudential Real Estate office. This was also the former office of Dr. William Makaroff, one of the town's two physicians, and was later converted to a laundromat and, later still, the River Reader bookstore. The First Street Community Church belfry is on the left. (Photograph by Valerie Munthe; collection of John C. Schubert.)

This view is east along Main Street, with the earlier image taken in 1940. Safeway was established here in 1937 and exists today at the west end of town. Towering behind the Chevron station is the Bank of Guerneville, built around 1920. Left of the speed limit sign was a bakery, now River Reader bookstore. To the right, where the original cement sidewalk ended, was the Greyhound bus station, now Vine Life shop. (Photograph by Jesse Munthe; collection of John C. Schubert.)

In this view north down Mill Street during the 1914 flood, Guidotti's Garibaldi Hotel sits to the left, currently the site of Buck's Restaurant, located at the corner of Fourth and Mill Streets. The residence on the right was formerly Hetzel's residence, then Hetzel's Resort, and is now the Russian River Resort. The lowest elevation in town, this area has a tendency to be the first to flood. (Photograph by Jesse Munthe; collection of John C. Schubert.)

This photograph is looking east up Fourth Street at St. Elizabeth's Catholic Church, originally built in 1905 and rebuilt in 1938. The steeple on the original building was bought from the Sebastopol Catholic Church. The building on the left is now the Russian River Fire Protection District office. The house to the right of the church was torn down to build the first firehouse, now used as storage for the fire district. (Photograph by Valerie Munthe; collection of John C. Schubert.)

Looking east up First Street from today's Safeway parking lot, the old Community Church, built in 1905, is on the right while today's Mill Street runs parallel to the white gate and fence, which encompasses the Westover Mansion (at the far right). The white building in the modern photograph houses Koala's Sushi Café and Mi Casita Mexican Restaurant, while directly behind it remains the church. (Photograph by Valerie Munthe; collection of John C. Schubert.)

The 1935 photograph shows a western view of John T. Coon's blacksmith shop, located on the west side of Armstrong Woods Road between Third and Fourth Streets, directly across from Coffee Bazaar. In the time between this photograph and 2010, Hil Grunberg's Signal gasoline station and auto repair shop resided at this spot, now the site of Russian River Vintage Travel Trailers and Steve's Foreign Auto. (Photograph by Jesse Munthe; collection of John C. Schubert.)

HEART OF THE RIVER: GUERNEVILLE AND GUERNEWOOD PARK

This postcard, dated 1916, illustrates the last Guerneville train station. After rail service ended in 1935, the building became Jack Luttrell's Meat Market, then was torn down in the mid-1960s. It is now the site of what locals know as the "B of A" building, which houses a variety of offices, including professional and community services. (Photograph by Jesse Munthe; collection of John C. Schubert.)

The earlier photograph was taken in 1950 and shows the first gas station at the southeast corner of Second and Mill Streets (now Main and Mill Streets). "Rip" Larner's Full-Service Union 76 Gas Station later became Stan Walker's Union 76. This second station was torn down in 1998, and the present owners Frank and Nancy Lambert completed construction of the third gas station on the site in 1999. (Photograph by Jesse Munthe; courtesy of the Ben Larner Collection.)

HEART OF THE RIVER: GUERNEVILLE AND GUERNEWOOD PARK

The 1913 photograph shows the northern view of one of the first areas cut by loggers, located west of downtown Guerneville. Gigantic redwood stumps were removed, and the land was used as a dairy farm. Due to annual flooding, the field over time became a vacant lot. Today it is now one of the various active vineyards owned and operated by Korbel Champagne Cellars. (Photograph by Valerie Munthe; collection of John C. Schubert.)

The Surrey Inn was known as the "finest in resort living on the Russian River," according to the back of this 1960s postcard. This popular resort was located in what is now a vacant lot of blackberry bushes, just west of downtown Guerneville. Built in 1946, the property experienced seasonal winter flooding almost every year until it was condemned and torn down and the property left vacant. (Photograph by Valerie Munthe; collection of John C. Schubert.)

HEART OF THE RIVER: GUERNEVILLE AND GUERNEWOOD PARK

Ferngrove Cottages, situated at the far west end of Guerneville on Highway 116, was originally constructed in 1920. The original office building burned down and was replaced with a two-story office/apartment building. Ferngrove is still in operation today as a popular spot for vacationers. The old grocery store is now the site of Taqueria La Tapatia Mexican Restaurant and Kaya Coffee Shop. (Photograph by Valerie Munthe; collection of John C. Schubert.)

This 1955 photograph shows the first Guerneville School building at the Armstrong Woods Road location. Constructed in 1949, this building and the old Jensen Hall erected in 1964 were torn down in the 1990s, when the school expanded from one to six permanent buildings. Because construction of the new Jensen Hall Multipurpose Room took roughly two years to complete (finished in 1997), students ate their lunches out in the play yard or in the classrooms. (Photograph by Valerie Munthe; collection of John C. Schubert.)

Charlie Wong's Good Food was the only Chinese restaurant in Guerneville in 1950. It was located 1 mile north of downtown at the corner of Armstrong and Watson Roads, now the site of the Russian River Senior Center. Typical of the era in a small town, Charlie Wong was the only Asian American on the river. His original back bar still exists inside the building. (Photograph by Valerie Munthe; collection of John C. Schubert.)

On Armstrong Road, 1 mile north of Guerneville, Calif.
Charlie Wong - Proprieto

This *c.* 1938 photograph shows the Administration Building constructed in 1935 in Armstrong Woods State Park. An indoor theater was located at the right end of the structure. From 1950 to 1952, the Stumptown Players performed here. One actress in the troupe, Carol Burnett, continued into big-time show business. The building was torn down in 1966, and in its place a forest has grown up. (Photograph by Valerie Munthe; collection of John C. Schubert.)

ADMINISTRATION BLDG. ARMSTRONG GROVE   R 12

Starting in 1934, the logs that were not used in the construction of the administration building for Armstrong Woods were instead used as benches and as stage reinforcement for the Redwood Theater. This theater was formally dedicated on September 27, 1936; an estimated 3,000 people attended. The log seats were replaced with wooden plank benches bolted to concrete in 1951. The amphitheater is still used for various activities, including the Old Grove Festival. (Photograph by Valerie Munthe; collection of John C. Schubert.)

Looking west towards Guernewood Park around 1912, the earlier photograph was taken just west of Ferngrove Cottages. The railroad tracks were converted into Highway 12 (later Highway 116) in 1936. A county access road, to the right, was the original pedestrian and wagon access into Guernewood Park and later ceased to be part of the highway along the river. (Photograph by Valerie Munthe; collection of John C. Schubert.)

HEART OF THE RIVER: GUERNEVILLE AND GUERNEWOOD PARK

Waiting for their train around 1912, vacationers heading home are photographed here, facing east towards Guerneville from Guernewood Park. The railway was originally built for logging in 1881 and later focused on passenger transportation beginning around 1900. The modern day Dubrava Village condominiums are located behind the viewer as Hulbert Creek flows behind the telephone pole from left to right. Today's Highway 116 has replaced the railroad tracks. (Photograph by Valerie Munthe; collection of John C. Schubert.)

Looking north, what is now Old Monte Rio Road, which connected pedestrian, wagon, and automobile traffic with Monte Rio and Guernewood Park, was also known as the Monte Rio Highway. The gated "To The Height" entrance to a summer homes development is now the intersection of Lover's Lane. (Photograph by Jesse Munthe; collection of John C. Schubert.)

ENTRANCE TO GUERNEWOOD PARK, GUERNEVILLE CAL.

Beneath the Towering Redwoods stands Guernewood Tavern

The *c.* 1938 photograph shows the entrance to the beach for Guernewood Park residents and vacationers. It is today known as Dubrava Beach. The Guernewood Tavern was built around 1905 but was originally a dance pavilion. At the time of the earlier photograph, this was the largest (some 14-plus acres) resort on the Russian River. (Photograph by Valerie Munthe; collection of John C. Schubert.)

As in 1940, this beach (now Dubrava Beach) is still very popular amongst the local and vacationing youth. Seen on its south side from Neeley Road, the Guernewood Park Tavern was later abandoned, vandalized, and burned down about 1974. There was no effort to rebuild until the development of Dubrava Village condominiums in the 1980s. (Photograph by Valerie Munthe; collection of John C. Schubert.)

HEART OF THE RIVER: GUERNEVILLE AND GUERNEWOOD PARK

Looking east at the Guernewood Park Sportsmen's Club with Highway 12 (now Highway 116) to the left, the tavern is to the right, Hulbert Creek runs behind, and Dubrava Village sits behind the photographer. Constructed in 1947, this building houses, from left to right, a grocery store, a bakery, a bar, and a restaurant. Torn down in the late 1960s, it gave way to an empty lot that exists today on the site. (Photograph by Valerie Munthe; collection of John C. Schubert.)

This northward 1940s view shows Guernewood Village; another vacation hot spot along the river, Hulbert Creek, runs behind it. Beyond the front of the cars is the entrance to an amusement walk where visitors could find a café, game booths (including Skee-Ball and a baseball throw with milk bottles), and so forth. Underneath the Guernewood Village sign is a grocery store. Just out of view to the right is today's Garden Grill. (Photograph by Jesse Munthe; collection of John C. Schubert.)

HEART OF THE RIVER: GUERNEVILLE AND GUERNEWOOD PARK

Just inside the entrance to Guernewood Village (built in the mid-1920s) was the Guernewood Grocery, known from the 1940s to the mid-1950s as Noble's Grocery Store. In 1962 to 1963, the building was razed and converted into a residence by Bill and Mary Lloyd, owners of Bill's Taxi Service. (Photograph by Valerie Munthe; collection of John C. Schubert.)

FERNEWOOD VILLAGE COMMUNITY CLUB HOUSE

In this *c.* 1929 image, just beyond the grocery store and game booths stands a dance pavilion, which was later converted into a roller-skating rink. Next to the rink (in order) are a café, pool hall, four-lane bowling alley, and the community clubhouse, last known as Molly Brown's Bar. In the open area in front of the clubhouse, free movies were shown in the evenings followed by a campfire. (Photograph by Valerie Munthe; collection of John C. Schubert.)

HEART OF THE RIVER: GUERNEVILLE AND GUERNEWOOD PARK

This 1954 photograph shows Sunday service being conducted at the Guernewood Park open-air church, located on Lover's Lane (to the left) alongside Hulbert Creek (to the right), with the Guernewood amusements just across the creek to the right. The church sold the property in the early 2000s, and it is now a privately owned vacant lot. (Photograph by Jesse Munthe; collection of John C. Schubert.)

CATHOLIC CHURCH
UNDER THE REDWOODS
GUERNE WOOD PARK CALIF.

The *c.* 1925 photograph is of the Monterosa Resort. It was located 1.5 miles up Old Cazadero Road in Hulbert Canyon on a natural, open flat. Due to typhoid contamination of the local water source, Monterosa Resort closed after two years of operation. The area, sometimes called "Out Fern Way," was developed in the 1960s by realtor Jack Wright as a summer and year-round residence neighborhood. (Photograph by Valerie Munthe; collection of John C. Schubert.)

CHAPTER 3

AROUND THE BEND TO THE RIVER'S END

MONTE RIO, DUNCANS MILLS, JENNER

The view from many homes built along the Russian River, such as this one, makes the area a remarkably beautiful place to escape to. This porch is part of the old Moscow Hotel, located on Moscow Road between Villa Grande and Duncans Mills. (Collection of John C. Schubert.)

VACATION BEACH
GUERNEVILLE, CALIF
LARK PHOTO

This *c.* 1930 photograph of Vacation Beach was taken from Summit Road in Guernewood Heights looking southeast. The land slowly developed from agricultural use into summer and residential homesites. Not seen in the earlier photograph but shown in the modern image is the summer crossing, a seasonal bridge that opens for the vacation season. The redwood forest growth is indicative of the time difference, as depicted in the current photograph, with modern-day Vacation Beach lying behind redwood trees. (Photograph by Valerie Munthe; collection of John C. Schubert.)

The area known as Greystone, located west of Guernewood Park along Highway 116, was named for the large gray boulder that rested in the Russian River, as seen in the 1910 photograph. The railroad tracks were removed in 1936, and State Highway 116 has taken their place. The mountainside above the railroad was carved away and used as fill for the roadbed of the highway. (Photograph by Jesse Munthe; collection of John C. Schubert.)

TURNER PHOTO.

NEAR GRAYSTONE—GUERNEVILLE, CAL.

As seen in the mid-1920s photographs, McClearie's was a popular train stop for vacationers to Greystone and Russian River Heights (now Old Monte Rio Road). During the 1940s and 1950s, the building was Hatcher's Store, which was torn down in the mid-1980s. The earlier photograph was taken during the summer just after a train departure, as depicted by the swim attire, overcoats, and suitcases of McClearie's patrons. (Photograph by Jesse Munthe; collection of John C. Schubert.)

21
il time at McClearies
ontesano- Cal.

Located roughly halfway between Northwood and Guernewood Park, this property, originally McClearie's, has changed little: to Ripken's Inn and then in 1965 to Angie and Geo's Hideaway. The area between the building and the highway, where the porch was, has been filled in. Today there is a small grove of redwoods there. (Photograph by Valerie Munthe; collection of John C. Schubert.)

Looking upriver in 1912, the view shows the Vacation Beach Crossing, also known as the "Lower Dam." The Vacation Beach Crossing continues to serve as a summertime shortcut to the south side of Russian River from Highway 116 (downriver from Greystone), as well as a public boat and beach access point. (Photograph by Kelly Ann Johnson; collection of John C. Schubert.)

This railroad business car, in the c. 1920 image, is parked in an area known as Northwood, just 3 miles west of Guerneville. This was the end of the standard-gage Guerneville branch of the Northwest Pacific Railroad. Northwood Golf Course is out of the view to the right. Old Monte Rio Road, which was the main highway until 1936, slopes uphill to the left of the car. (Photograph by Valerie Munthe; collection of John C. Schubert.)

Bob and Edith's Union 76 Gas Station, pictured here during the 1940 flood, was the grocery and supply store for residents on the north side of the river in Monte Rio. In 1960, Fern Gambetta bought the store, and it has been known as "Fern's" ever since. The gas pumps were removed in 1998. (Photograph by Valerie Munthe; collection of John C. Schubert.)

This photograph, taken in 1940, is of Bartlette's grocery store, which still exists and is the primary store for residents of Monte Rio. The building to the left of Bartlette's was a bakery and is now the intersection of Main Street and Moscow Road. The building at far left was the railroad freight warehouse. The area is now the Sonoma County Transit Park 'n Ride at the bottom of Starrett Hill. (Photograph by Valerie Munthe; collection of John C. Schubert.)

The vacationer to Monte Rio would ride the narrow-gage railroad through Occidental and arrive at the station seen on the left in this 1905 photograph of Main Street. Typical of summer, Chinese lanterns (seen on the building above to the right) were strung up at the resorts and summer homes. The buildings to the right today are Berger's Construction and the Monte Rio Fire Protection District's auxiliary firehouse. (Photograph by Valerie Munthe; collection of John C. Schubert.)

An afternoon train arrives in 1908 from Duncans Mills over what is now Moscow Road. It will go up Dutch Bill Creek towards Occidental and points south. Behind the station, Starrett Hill Road heads uphill. The Monte Rio Hotel, to the left, was torn down in 1935 and replaced by the Starrett Hill Road retaining wall. The Monte Rio Fire Department is located just to the left of the old hotel site. (Photograph by Valerie Munthe; collection of John C. Schubert.)

The older photograph shows the bustling metropolis of Monte Rio in 1940. From left to right are the Pink Elephant Bar, Nicleas' ("Nickels") Bungalow Café, the entrance to the Monte Rio Amphitheater, Torr's Coffee Shop, Odell's Grocery Store, the Monte Rio Post Office, and Lee Torr Jr.'s Real Estate and Insurance. Today only the Pink Elephant remains. (Photograph by Jesse Munthe; collection of John C. Schubert.)

View at Montrio. Sonoma Co., Cal.   NO. SHORE RR
MONTE RIO STA.

MONTE RIO

Looking south from the perspective of the previous image is the Russell Hotel, seen at the center. To the left of the station is the semaphore (train signal) telling trains in both directions to stop at the station. The Monte Rio Hotel sits behind the train station. This is now the site of Sonoma County Transit Park and Ride. (Photograph by Valerie Munthe; collection of John C. Schubert.)

Pictured in this *c.* 1945 photograph is Angelo's Resort, also known as Angelo's Casino. Owned then by Angelo Torre, it was located on River Boulevard, a half-mile east of Monte Rio. The casino is now a private home, known and marked as "Grandma's House," and the cabins are now used as residences. (Photograph by Jesse Munthe; collection of John C. Schubert.)

The 1915 photograph, looking southeast, shows the north side of Monte Rio long before it was developed. The canyon in the center background (seen below), called Madrone Mill Creek, leads to Bohemian Grove, a famous private men's club. Dead center in the earlier photograph is the modern location of Fern's Market on Highway 116. The beach in the foreground is the present-day Monte Rio Public Beach. (Photograph by Jesse Munthe; collection of John C. Schubert.)

VIEW FROM PORCH SULLY'S MONTE RIO CAL.

Looking southwest at Starrett Hill, the railroad right-of-way (today's Moscow Road) runs along the far bank just above the bridge. When the footbridge in this 1915 photograph was removed, the upper portions of the pilings were cut, and the remaining stumps are still visible today under the surface of the water, as depicted by the beachgoers in the modern photograph. Behind the footbridge to the left is the Monte Rio Public Beach. (Photograph by Valerie Munthe; collection of John C. Schubert.)

Shown here in 1909, Big Sandy Beach was *the* beach in Monte Rio. This location, on the north side of the river, is now owned by Monte Rio Recreation and Parks District and is the site of a public boat-launching ramp. The current Monte Rio Public Beach is 100 yards to the right of this view (upstream). (Photograph by Jesse Munthe; collection of John C. Schubert.)

A rare moment taken during construction of the new and current Monte Rio Bridge in 1934 shows the two spans side by side. The older bridge, on the right, was built in 1914 but became outdated due to an increase in automobile traffic. The north ends of both bridges (behind the viewer) are located in front of today's Rio Theater. The south end of the old bridge terminated just east of Barlett's Store. (Photograph by Valerie Munthe; collection of John C. Schubert.)

Taken during a lull of the flood of 1937, this view is looking north from Monte Rio Bridge up Church Street towards St. Catherine's Catholic Church. The Shell station site, located to the right on a triangular piece of land, is now a parking lot across from the Rio Theater (above, to the right, not pictured). The current entrance to the public beach is off to the left. (Photograph by Jesse Munthe; collection of John C. Schubert.)

Today facing west towards Duncans Mills, this main highway, located on the south side of the Russian River, was originally the route for the narrow-gage North Pacific Coast Railroad. When the Northwestern Pacific Railroad bought the narrow gage (the rail in the middle), the company laid standard-gage rail next to it, on the right. The railroad withdrew from the river in 1935, and the right-of-way became Moscow Road. (Photograph by Valerie Munthe; collection of John C. Schubert.)

MESA GRANDE

Villa Grande was originally known as Mesa Grande (meaning "big table"), then Grandeville in 1907, and finally Villa Grande in 1921. After logging ceased, the small community had its own hotel and post office with general store and gas station. It was a flag stop on the North Pacific Coast narrow-gage railroad. (Photograph by Valerie Munthe; collection of John C. Schubert.)

The North Pacific Coast Railroad crossed the Russian River at Duncans Mills and traveled up today's Moscow Road towards Monte Rio. This bridge has been replaced three times. The first span, built of wood in 1890, had piers knocked out by a flood and was torn down in 1917; the second, a steel girder railroad bridge, was later torn down; and the third, made of concrete, is what exists today. Behind the bridge is the Casini Ranch Family Campground. (Photograph by Valerie Munthe; collection of John C. Schubert.)

This is Duncans Mills looking north on B Street (formerly part of the old highway going to Jenner) around 1912. The home on the left is the DeCarly residence, which was relocated behind the general store. The railroad tracks ran from Monte Rio and Guerneville through Duncans Mills to Cazadero. Part of this route is currently Highway 116. (Photograph by Valerie Munthe; collection of John C. Schubert.)

Main Street Duncan's Mills, Cal

Originally known as the Scotta School District, this building was the school's second location, the first being near Jenner. Duncans Mills, a small community now, had sufficient population to warrant its own school. The schoolhouse was built around 1880 and shut down in 1950–1951. What remains today is this condemned structure above. (Photograph by Valerie Munthe; collection of John C. Schubert.)

The ferry in the earlier photograph was the only means for a vehicle to cross the Russian River and travel south on Coast Highway 1 to Bodega Bay. This ferry crossing was in operation for about 60-plus years; it was the first ferry north of San Francisco. Upon completion of the Coast Highway 1 Bridge in 1933, the ferry was towed to the middle of the river and burned. (Photograph by Jesse Munthe; collection of John C. Schubert.)

Travelers would no longer need to wait for the ferry. This is the celebration of the opening of the Coast Highway 1 Bridge at Jenner, now known as Bridgehaven. Built during the height of the Depression by the Works Progress Administration (WPA), this bridge was paramount at the time because it permitted a continuous flow of traffic by connecting the north and south banks of the Russian River. (Photograph by Valerie Munthe; collection of John C. Schubert.)

The town of Jenner, first established as a lumber mill site built in 1904, is located at the mouth of the Russian River. In 1914, "Jenner By The Sea" was deemed by the *Press Democrat* a full-fledged resort area, housing few residents and many vacationers. Over time the rate of residents grew, and along with the remaining vacation homes and two prominent restaurants, the Jenner Inn and River's End, Jenner continues its reputation as a premier Sonoma Coast destination. (Photograph by Jesse Munthe; collection of John C. Schubert.)

Jenner by the Sea, constructed in 1904, was the main town building, housing the general store, post office, restaurant, and bar. It later burned in 1948. The 1949 rebuild was designed by a Julia Morgan understudy architect and constructed by boatbuilders Fred Mecum and Cecil Mecum Jr. with help from the townspeople. Richard Murphy has owned the restaurant and inn since 1979. (Photograph by Jesse Munthe; collection of John C. Schubert.)

Looking northwest at the mouth of the Russian River, the rudimentary Coast Highway 1 meanders along the hillside to the right. Where the original pier stood is now a public nonmotorized boat access, owned by California State Parks. Here boaters and kayakers get to experience an array of wildlife, including river otter, seals, and bioluminescent plankton. (Photograph by Jesse Munthe; collection of John C. Schubert.)

Mouth of Russian River
301   Bartlett Photo

Work started on this jetty in 1929, two years before this photograph was made. Due to lack of funds, the site was reclaimed by the ocean. Rock for the jetty was hauled via railroad from Goat Rock. The railway equipment came from the Twin Peaks Tunnel construction in San Francisco. A section of the jetty and rails is still visible on the beach, a part of the Sonoma Coast State Parks. (Photograph by Valerie Munthe; collection of John C. Schubert.)

Until the 1920s, Goat Rock was an island. In 1929, the east face of the rock was converted into a quarry to supply materials for the Jenner jetty. The rocks from the quarry also provided the base for the parking lot that exists there today. Now part of the California State Parks system, Goat Rock State Beach is a popular destination for beachgoers. (Photograph by Valerie Munthe; collection of John C. Schubert.)

OCEAN. MOUTH RUSSIAN RIVER. RHEA. Ent.

DISCOVER THOUSANDS OF LOCAL HISTORY BOOKS
FEATURING MILLIONS OF VINTAGE IMAGES

Arcadia Publishing, the leading local history publisher in the United States, is committed to making history accessible and meaningful through publishing books that celebrate and preserve the heritage of America's people and places.

Find more books like this at
www.arcadiapublishing.com

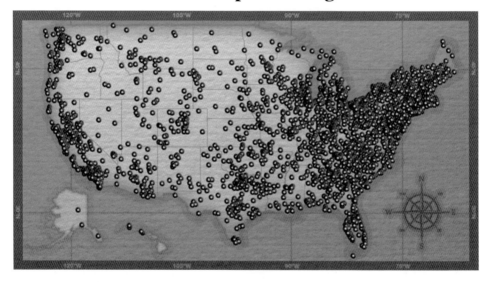

Search for your hometown history, your old stomping grounds, and even your favorite sports team.